Original title:
Ferns and Fantasies

Copyright © 2025 Creative Arts Management OÜ
All rights reserved.

Author: Rafael Sterling
ISBN HARDBACK: 978-1-80581-792-5
ISBN PAPERBACK: 978-1-80581-319-4
ISBN EBOOK: 978-1-80581-792-5

Ephemeral Shades of Enchantment

In a jungle of dreams, I found a frog,
Dancing on leaves and wearing a smog.
It wore a top hat and twirled with glee,
Singing of biscuits and hot cups of tea.

Beneath the moonlight, shadows all play,
A squirrel in slippers steals snacks on the way.
Wise old owls chuckle from branches above,
As the grasshoppers hum a tune full of love.

The Lure of Leafy Labyrinths

With vines like ribbons, they twist and they twirl,
Rabbits in waistcoats around me they whirl.
They offer me carrots in pockets they hide,
As I tumble and giggle on this leafy ride.

A map made of lettuce uncovers the path,
Leading to giggles and rosy-faced wrath.
With mischievous whispers, the pathways conspire,
To send me spinning into a ring of fire!

Fantastical Fernlight

Beneath the soft glow of vibrant green light,
Dance little beetles, a waltz in the night.
They bump and they tumble, they laugh as they sway,
In a party of nature, they jest and they play.

The glowworms are DJing with beats so absurd,
While ladybugs break dance, oh, how they are heard!
With twinkling wings they flutter about,
Turning the forest to a wild night out.

Elven Footprints on Mossy Floors

Elves in the glen leave prints oh so light,
Chasing their shadows, they giggle in flight.
They trip on the mushrooms and land with delight,
Throwing confetti of petals in sight.

A twist of the wrist, and a dance in the air,
Raindrops like jewels, they toss without care.
With laughter that sparkles and echoes through trees,
They whisper their secrets to playful old bees.

The Path of Verdant Whimsy

In the glen where green socks play,
Frogs wear crowns, hip-hop on hay.
Snails boast about their long, gooey trails,
While bushes gossip and sway with tales.

A dandelion sneezes, sends spores on a spree,
Chasing rabbits who laugh with glee.
Toadstools twirl in a jig by the brook,
While crickets compose songs in a storybook.

Butterflies argue over floral real estate,
As bees buzz in suits, it's a floral debate.
The wind teases leaves in a tickling spree,
Which way to dance? Oh, let them be!

So join the parade in this mischievous woods,
Where giggles sprout up like laughter in buds.
In this joyful chaos, let your spirit soar,
For nature's a circus with fun at its core.

Dreams Spun in Nature's Embrace

In a meadow of laughter and chirps so bright,
A squirrel dons shades, what a funny sight!
He hosts a tea party under the old oak,
With acorns as cups—oh, that's no joke!

Dragonflies wear capes, swooping and gliding,
While daisies do cartwheels, giggling beside him.
A ladybug sports a polka-dot dress,
And claims all the flowers—the ultimate mess!

The clouds in the sky play hide and seek,
Tickling the trees, making them squeak.
With a gust of the breeze, laughter takes flight,
As the sun hiccups loudly, what a delight!

So dance with the dandelions, twirl in the sky,
Join the chorus of nature, don't be shy.
For in this wild world of joy and embrace,
Every twist and turn brings a smile to your face.

The Secret Life of Lush Fronds

In the garden, whispers grow,
Lively secrets, a show of woe.
Swaying softly, a leafy jest,
Who knew they had such fun at rest?

They throw parties with the breeze,
Tickled by the buzzing bees.
Talking tales of sun and rain,
While playing hide and seek in vain.

Sylvan Dreams in the Moonlight

Underneath the silver glow,
Nibbling snacks, the critters show.
With shadows long, they toss and twirl,
Dancing plants in a leafy whirl.

A raccoon in a hat so grand,
Seems to lead a merry band.
With twinkling eyes and silly feet,
At the party, they can't be beat.

Veil of Verdant Mysteries

Secrets lie in green disguise,
Behind each leaf, a watchful eye.
Giggling roots stretch far and wide,
Making mischief where they hide.

The froggy choir sings so bright,
As fireflies buzz through the night.
With jokes exchanged in leafy lines,
Nature's jesters with secret signs.

The Dance of the Hidden Ones

In tangled paths, they skip and slide,
With creeping vines, they run and hide.
Caterpillars move in time,
To a rhythm, oh so prime!

With giggles flitting on the air,
They play tricks without a care.
Each twist and turn's a secret game,
Whispers floating, calling names.

Woods of Whimsy

In the woods where giggles hide,
Trees wear hats, and squirrels guide.
Butterflies dance in silly loops,
Chasing shadows of tiny troops.

Frogs in coats croak out of tune,
While mushrooms play a game at noon.
Breezes whisper cheeky jokes,
As nature's laughter softly strokes.

Bugs in glasses, looking sly,
Compete in races, oh my, oh my!
Each leaf drips with playful cheer,
While woods echo the joy we hear.

The Hidden Tapestry of Nature

A fabric woven through the trees,
Where raccoons plot to swipe some cheese.
The flowers chuckle, petals fanned,
Roots tangle up in a merry band.

The brook giggles, splashes bright,
Making fish jump in sheer delight.
Clouds float by with silly faces,
Creating rainbows in wild places.

Ants in suits march to a beat,
On tiny paths, they rarely meet.
Nature's quilt, so weird and fun,
Stitches stories for everyone!

Mystical Tendrils of Growth

In gardens where the gnomes collide,
Vines twist up with goofy pride.
Worms wear shades in the cool damp earth,
Counting blessings, knowing worth.

Sunlight tickles each green sprout,
As ladybugs dance all about.
Toads recite their ribbit tales,
While plants put on their quirky veils.

The breeze carries jokes of the day,
As petals sway and play their way.
Nature's riddle in layers deep,
Laughter wakes the world from sleep.

A Canvas of Green Dreams

In a canvas brushed with shades of spree,
Laughter ripples through every tree.
Colors splash in a joyous mess,
Even the bees seem to dress to impress.

Pinecones giggle as they fall,
While grasses whisper tales to all.
Each twig adorned with a playful wink,
As squirrels debate what they should think.

Marshmallows in clouds float so high,
While dandelions bid the world goodbye.
Each dream painted in hues so keen,
Wakes laughter in this vibrant scene.

Secrets Woven in Fronds

In a garden where shadows play,
Leaves giggle at the break of day.
A squirrel dons a leafy hat,
He curses 'bout his missing cat!

Lizards dance on crooked logs,
While snails debate with rambunctious frogs.
The moon's a friend, a joker too,
As whispers weave through morning dew.

The Green Dreamers' Haven

In a realm where green does thrive,
Sleeping gnomes hold their jive.
A songbird croons a silly tune,
As rabbits hop 'neath the bright moon.

Mushrooms wear their poppy hats,
While fairies tease the chirping bats.
The grass plays tricks, it tickles toes,
And in the breeze, a laughter flows.

The Whispering Wildwood

In the wildwood where chatter's rife,
Trees gossip about woodland life.
A chipmunk juggles acorns with flair,
While he swears he saw a dragon there!

Crickets wear squeaky shoes that squeal,
Raccoons ponder their next big meal.
The canopy dances, then drips with cheer,
As shadows hide from the cuter deer.

The Enigma of Leafy Lores

In a thicket full of dreams untold,
Mysteries linger, both brave and bold.
A wise old owl spins tales of yore,
While squirrels giggle at an ancient war.

Vines curl up to share a laugh,
About a frog's failed climbing craft.
Echoes bounce from tree to tree,
As the forest bursts with giggly glee.

Memories Woven with Fronds

In the garden, creatures dance,
A squirrel twirls in a fancy pants.
The shadows giggle in leafy glee,
While snails debate their ancestry.

Laughter bubbles in the breeze,
As bugs take turns on mini skis.
A hedgehog sings a tune so loud,
The daisies bow, they're quite too proud.

Toadstools clap with tiny hands,
And rabbits form their marching bands.
With every rustle, stories unfold,
Of leafy dreams and treasures gold.

So grab your hat, and join the fun,
In this wild world, there's room for one!
With hidden tales in every twist,
You'll laugh so much, you'll feel a mist.

Delicate Sagas of Sprout and Light

Underneath where shadows play,
Whimsical tales come out to sway.
A gnome with shoes a size too small,
Tripped on roots and made a call.

The butterflies wore crowns of flair,
Challenging bees for buzzing air.
As waltzing petals hit the floor,
Ants served snacks—there's always more!

A mushroom suddenly wore a dress,
It swayed and spun—it was a mess!
The ladybugs cheered, "What a sight!"
"More parties needed!" echoed the night.

With giggles in every dampened nook,
And secrets whispered by each brook:
These playful moments twirl and twine,
In a world where even weeds can shine.

Leafy Tales of Lore and Legend

In a patch where leafy chats ignite,
The critters gather, all dressed right.
A parrot claims to know the way,
As raccoons sip on juice and play.

A turtle with a crown so bold,
Tells a story that never gets old.
"Once I raced a speedy sprout,
And you won't believe what it's about!"

Spiders weave their silky threads,
While frogs compete in comfy beds.
A banquet spread on tiny boughs,
Hosts giggles from the greenest cows.

With chittering thoughts and nuts to munch,
Creativity flows at every crunch.
In this realm of twisting vines,
Who wouldn't laugh at truly fine designs?

Enchantment Beneath the Sylvan Canopy

Beneath the trees where whispers twine,
Excited critters sip sweet wine.
A squirrel juggles acorns with flair,
While wise old owls spin tales in air.

The shadows waltz upon the ground,
As funky mushrooms start to sound.
"I'm the king of this leafy scene!"
Proclaims a pesky, peckish bean.

A raccoon with a guitar plays,
Strumming beats that catch the rays.
The forest fills with laughter's spark,
As night begins to bring out the dark.

Curious crickets start a band,
With shaking leaves, they make a stand.
In this tapestry of green and light,
The fun continues through the night.

Whispers of the Undergrowth

In the jungle where giggles grow,
Lizards wear hats, putting on a show.
Beetles dance in their shiny shoes,
While snails debate the best flavors of stews.

The trees gossip about their old leaves,
Tickling the breeze with small, playful heaves.
A rabbit jumps rope with a clever old toad,
In a world where laughter is the motherlode.

Enchanted Greenery

Mice in tuxedos, sipping on dew,
Plotting mischief in a grand leafy zoo.
A squirrel juggles acorns with flair,
While frogs sing operas as if they're rare.

The flowers throw parties, their colors ablaze,
While blossoms impersonate wizards' gaze.
Dancing to rhythms of the buzzing bees,
Life's a comedy, floated on the breeze.

Shadows Beneath the Canopy

In shadows, where shadows conjure delight,
A raccoon debates if it's day or night.
The owls roll their eyes, "Take a nap, friend,"
As the sunbeams giggle, they twist and bend.

A crab wearing glasses tries to read leaves,
Complaining that nature's a puzzle that deceives.
Bats in bow ties hold a gala so grand,
While ants march around with a tiny marching band.

Dreamweaver among the Leaves

In a world where whispers dream and play,
A dandelion dons a crown made of hay.
With twinkling eyes, the springs come alive,
Bartering giggles for dreams that survive.

The wind is a jester with jokes to unfold,
Telling tales of the brave and the bold.
Mushrooms giggle as they sprout all around,
In a wild, wacky show that knows no bounds.

The Celestial Fernscape

In the forest of thoughts, where giggles rise,
A plant with a wink and mischievous eyes.
It dances with breezes, oh what a sight,
Even the stars chuckle, tucked in at night.

With leaves shaped like hats, they tip and they sway,
As if greeting squirrels, saying, "Come play!"
The moon hums a tune, a whimsical beat,
While shadows perform with their tiny green feet.

Every frond tells a tale, in whispers so sly,
Like secrets of laughter that flutter on by.
It teases the gnomes, the garden's brigade,
Who trip over roots as their mischief parade.

Oh, the antics they share in this leafy delight,
As critters convene for a frolic at night.
A comedy show where the wild things convene,
In a realm where the funny is always unseen.

The Green Labyrinth of Dreams

In a maze made of laughter, all covered in moss,
The creatures hold meetings, discussing their floss.
A rabbit with glasses, stout and quite wise,
Proclaims, "We're all fables, like bees or like pies!"

They weave through the paths, with a spring in their hop,
Avoiding the spots where the daisies might flop.
A toad on a lily, wearing shoes made of clay,
Jumps high just to show he can dance anyway!

The mushrooms are grinning, adorned with fine hats,
While hedgehogs recite their old jokes to the bats.
With every twist, turn, and the giggles that merge,
The laughter grows louder, as silliness surge.

When morning arrives, with birds ready to croon,
They part ways, promising a meet under moon.
For in this green puzzle, where whimsy resides,
The joy of the journey is where humor hides.

Whimsy Amongst the Greenery

In the thicket of chuckles, where sunbeams collide,
A snail with a top hat takes flowers in stride.
Hopping around, a grasshopper sings,
"Why don't we make music with all kinds of things?"

The daisies all giggle, they wiggle with glee,
They join in the fun, and they sway to the spree.
A caterpillar bursts forth with sparkles and flair,
"I'm just a slow dancer, don't mind me, I swear!"

A squirrel juggles acorns, all polished and round,
While the brook plays a tune, with a giggly sound.
They frolic and tumble, no worries in sight,
In this patch of mishaps, mischief takes flight.

At dusk, when the critters all gather around,
They share all their blunders, as laughter's unbound.
For in this green haven, where joy is a scheme,
Even the tallest of oaks wants to join in the dream.

Enchanted Growths of the Wild

In the wilds where the humor grows tall as a tree,
A bush starts to chuckle, quite jolly, you'll see.
Each frond waves hello, with a grin and a cheer,
While the crickets proclaim, "Let's all hold our beer!"

A flower with sunglasses lounges in shade,
Winks at a dragonfly, a prank on parade.
A jolly old owl, with a twinkle in eye,
Says, "What's life without giggles and a bit of pie?"

The ants form a band, with their crumbs for a drum,
And dance to the rhythm of all that's been spun.
They carol through the night, making merry and cheer,
While the stars come to listen, intrigued and sincere.

So gather your giggles, let nonsense take flight,
In the heart of this wild, everything feels right.
For in every sprout's laughter, a joy to behold,
Life's magic is found in the stories retold.

The Language of Leaves

Whispers rustle through the trees,
A giggle from a sneaky breeze.
Leaves are chatting, soft and sly,
Secret jokes as clouds float by.

Beneath the shade, a squirrel grins,
Telling tales with tiny spins.
Roots chuckle deep within the ground,
Life's a jest that's quite profound.

Dancing shadows play their part,
Nature's humor, a work of art.
Tickling petals, swaying air,
Who knew foliage had such flair?

So listen close, and you might find,
The playful hearts of leaves combined.
In every rustle, laugh and cheer,
Nature's jesters, always near.

Tales of the Fey in the Flora

In a thicket, sprites convene,
Tickling blooms, a vibrant scene.
With tiny hats and dancing shoes,
They sip on dew and share their muse.

Behind a toadstool, secrets flow,
Whispers catch the sunlight's glow.
A bee with stories, quick and bright,
Buzzes in, a buzzing sprite.

Petals giggle, twirl and spin,
As woodland critters join within.
With every leap and merry roll,
The fey keep merry, heart and soul.

Oh, to join their lively game,
To taste the joy, and share a name!
But keep it hush, for what they say,
Is meant for dancing, not for day.

Lullabies of the Hidden Canopy

Up above, a lullaby,
Chirping birds that flirt and fly.
Gentle beams on leaves do play,
A serenade to end the day.

Little frogs compose a tune,
Underneath the silver moon.
A waltz of shadows, soft and light,
As sleepy blooms bid day goodnight.

In the hush, the laughter's sweet,
As crickets tap their tiny feet.
Nature's choir, a merry blend,
Where jests and dreams will never end.

So close your eyes, and let it be,
A whimsical night of jubilee.
In slumber deep, the tales will weave,
The secrets of the eve, believe!

Emerald Brocade of the Dreaming Earth

On carpet green, they prance around,
Emerald threads adorn the ground.
A bashful bud peeks out to tease,
With charms that float upon the breeze.

Curly vines entwine in jest,
Playing tickle games, a quest.
In every nook, a critter grins,
With tangled tales and playful spins.

Amidst the glade, a humor fest,
Squirrels mimes in nature's jest.
They frolic on this vibrant stage,
Life unfolds its merry page.

So take a stroll, embrace the cheer,
In Nature's world, the fun is clear.
Dance with the leaves, and laugh along,
For every heart can sing a song.

Lush Dreams in Shade

In a world where leaves wear hats,
And dance around like silly cats,
The dappled light plays tricks on me,
Sipping tea from a mushroom spree.

A critter laughs beneath a frond,
Complaining life's a bit too fond,
Of sunny days and silly games,
While everyone forgets their names.

Tiny trolls with wings so bright,
Play tag beneath the moon's soft light,
While dew drops hide in cozy nooks,
And giggle over funny books.

Oh, what a joy to spin and twirl,
In this leafy, whimsical whirl,
Where shadows tease, and dreams collide,
In the laughter of the forest wide.

Sylvan Secrets Unveiled

Whispers rustle through the trees,
As squirrels perform their clumsy tease,
With acorns flying, oh what fun,
A nutty party just begun.

Bouncing mushrooms, one by one,
Say they're the life of every run,
While woodland shadows start to sing,
Of magic hats and silly bling.

An owl in glasses reads the news,
Excited by the latest views,
Of rabbits dancing in the rain,
While hedgehogs jog without a strain.

Joyful echoes fill the air,
From creatures who have no despair,
In this lush and lively spree,
Where all are wild and ever free.

The Enchanted Grove

A sleepy snail rides on a leaf,
Comically slow beyond belief,
While flowers giggle with delight,
At every curious, silly sight.

The fairies play a game of chase,
With pixie dust and silly grace,
Their tiny giggles fill the air,
As mushrooms watch without a care.

A beetle struts in shiny shoes,
Pretending he has fancy views,
While butterflies just roll their eyes,
At his attempts to win the prize.

In this grove of merry cheer,
Where laughter echoes far and near,
Nature's fun is on display,
In the most whimsical of ways.

Shadows of the Verdant Realm

In shadows deep, the fun begins,
Where laughter sparks and mischief spins,
A clever fox dons a cape so bright,
And leads the dance into the night.

The flowers gossip, bloom and sway,
Sharing secrets, come what may,
While ladybugs compete in grace,
To see who wins the dancing race.

A rocking chair made out of twigs,
Swings gently, teasing all the digs,
As crickets strum their tiny bands,
Creating tunes for shadowed hands.

Here in this realm where dreams take flight,
And whimsy paints the world so bright,
The joy of life can't be contained,
In this echo of the playful gained.

Enchantment in the Thicket

In a grove where giggles grow,
Leaves are dancing to and fro.
Squirrels tie their shoes with ease,
While rabbits argue 'bout the breeze.

A fox in glasses reads a tome,
His stories wander far from home.
The mushrooms chuckle in delight,
As shadows play in dappled light.

With fairies juggling acorns round,
And hedgehogs twirling on the ground,
A lighthearted ballet there,
In a hidden world beyond compare.

So join the jesters of the glade,
Where every leaf is softly swayed.
The thicket sings a merry tune,
As laughter bounces 'neath the moon.

Mystical Breezes through the Green

Among the leaves, a whisper sings,
Of clumsy squirrels and magical things.
The daisies giggle, tickled by rain,
While toads recite their jokes in vain.

A breeze that tosses hats away,
Makes even old owls want to play.
With winks and nudges shared around,
The humor spreads from ground to ground.

The sunbeams join, a playful crew,
Creating shadows just for you.
Twirling ferns like dancers prance,
In this splendid, cheeky dance.

So come, oh wanderer, take a chance,
Join the flora in their playful dance.
A world where laughter freely flows,
And the magic of mischief always grows.

Twilight Beneath the Boughs

In twilight hours, the laughter blooms,
From cozy nooks and hidden rooms.
With giggling grubs and winking snails,
The night unfolds its silly tales.

Chirping crickets play their song,
While glowworms join, they can't be wrong.
Their bioluminescent show,
Brightens paths where whimsy flows.

An owl's onstage with an old-wise grin,
Poking fun at where we've been.
Beneath the boughs, the fun ignites,
With every leaf, a new delight.

So let the dusk be filled with cheer,
With every rustle, fun draws near.
In the shadows where jesters play,
The twilight brings a grand ballet.

Whispers from the Moss

Beneath the moss where secrets dwell,
Giggling stones have tales to tell.
Each pebble shares a cheeky jest,
As mushrooms bounce in playful rest.

The woodpecker's tap is a funky beat,
While bunnies hop to a rhythmic feet.
In this quiet nook, fun takes flight,
With whispers tickling the starry night.

A snail with style, all in a suit,
Slides by in tales quite absolute.
His shell adorned with shiny flair,
Rousing smiles from creatures rare.

So linger a while, let laughter pounce,
In this enchanted, joyful bounce.
For every whisper, every cross,
Is filled with mirth from that green moss.

Echoes in the Underbrush

In the green where giggles grow,
A squirrel sings in tones so low.
Bouncing leaves like little clowns,
Tickling shadows all around.

A rabbit dons a silly hat,
While pondering just where he's at.
With every jump, a sassy twirl,
The woodland bursts with furry whirl.

When mushrooms start to sway and sway,
A deer proclaims it's dance day!
The bugs all gather round the show,
With twinkling lights in rows aglow.

Oh, frolic in this vibrant sphere,
Where laughter echoes, sweet and clear.
Nature's jesters, bold in hue,
Creating mischief just for you.

The Green Tapestry

In a patchwork quilt of emerald cheer,
Lies a tale that's ever near.
A dogwood laughs as it sways,
While a chipmunk plans a game of play.

The leaves wink down from heights above,
Sprinkling joy and twinkling love.
A garden party, nature's feast,
Buds and blooms, they thrived the least.

A snail in shades of glossy sheen,
Wonders if he's a racing machine.
With every inch, he squeaks and slides,
As bumbles bees cheer from the sides.

Beneath the dance of sunlight's ray,
The flora joins in wild ballet.
A tapestry of laughter spun,
In this grove, we all have fun.

Sprites Amongst the Leaves

Little sprites in leafy capes,
Flit and flutter like dancing grapes.
On branches swing with glee and gloat,
While the gusty winds take note.

With faerie dust that tickles tricks,
They whisper secrets, jump, and flick.
A poplar giggles, branches creak,
As playful sprites begin to sneak.

A dragonfly in polka dots,
Joins the party with silly trots.
Sipping nectar, what a sight,
As blossoms blush with pure delight.

In this realm where mischief reigns,
And laughter echoes through the lanes,
The smallest things bring joy complete,
Where nature's magic feels so sweet.

A Dance of Delicate Fronds

In the hush of shady green,
A dance unfolds, unseen, serene.
With dainty steps, the fronds arise,
Bowing down to nature's ties.

A hedgehog spins in bright array,
As crickets start to serenade.
Each leaf a partner, sways in tune,
Underneath the silver moon.

The groundhog twirls with stubby feet,
Chasing shadows, quick and fleet.
His pirouettes, a comic view,
While blooms applaud the wild debut.

In playful breeze, the show won't cease,
As nature spins her joy and peace.
Join the fray, come laugh and prance,
In this whimsical leaf-dance.

Beneath the Canopy of Hopes

Under the leafy arch we play,
A squirrel mocks us, what a day!
The sun peeks through with a cheeky grin,
Inviting all the mischief to begin.

The mushrooms giggle, all in a row,
Tickling toadstools, don't you know?
A bunny hops by, dressed in style,
Winking at the world with a fluffy smile.

A chattering bird joins the fun,
Quipping jokes that weigh a ton.
Each rustling leaf has quite the tale,
As laughter echoes through the vale.

So come on down, bring your cheer,
Beneath this green, we shed our fear.
In nature's court, we jest and twirl,
An enchanted land, our playful world.

The Mystic Labyrinth of Leaves

In a maze of green, I lost my way,
A raccoon laughed, 'You'll pay to play!'
Around each bend, surprises await,
With sprightly whispers from the gate.

The branches twist like a surreal dance,
Inviting us in for a quirky chance.
A frog recites poetry, quite absurd,
As butterflies laugh, not disturbed.

One turn leads to a tickling breeze,
That rustles softly through the trees.
A hedgehog sells dreams from a tiny stand,
Offering giggles, all carefully planned.

So wander freely, don't be shy,
Where the wiggly paths reach for the sky.
Embrace the whimsy, let your heart weave,
In this labyrinth where all can believe.

Harmonies in the Thicket

In the thicket, songs collide,
A symphony of critters, side by side.
The crickets chirp, a bustling beat,
While squirrels dance on nimble feet.

A dandelion whispers the news,
Of forest parties and playful ruse.
The snails hold meetings, slow and grand,
Discussing plans for a marching band.

A parody of leaves sings very loud,
Drawing in an unsuspecting crowd.
The flitting insects join the choir,
With harmonies that never tire.

So if you listen, you might just hear,
A melody born from silly cheer.
Gather 'round, let your spirits lift,
In this thicket of nature's gift.

The Secret Language of Greens

The greens are chatting, can you hear?
With secret whispers, drawing near.
A sage old fern with tales to tell,
Of mischievous elves who know them well.

Clover conspiracies swirl with glee,
While daisies pose for a selfie.
Each frond has its own clever quip,
In the playful banter, take a sip.

A gnarled tree chuckles with delight,
As shadows dance in fading light.
The whispers of leaves, a merry jest,
In this green world, we are blessed.

So let's join in and share our fun,
As nature's laughter fills the sun.
In a world where jokes run free,
The greens unite, so come and see.

Glimmers of Magic within the Green

In the shade where whispers play,
Dancing shadows on display.
Silly sprites with mischief bright,
Tickle toes in morning light.

Beneath a cloak of emerald hue,
Giggling faeries weave anew.
Jumping jests in every nook,
Tea with toadstools, take a look!

Invisible hats that spin and sway,
Invisible friends that laugh and play.
Catch a glimpse, don't run away,
Join the orchestra of the day!

So let your worries drift and twirl,
Join the dance, give joy a whirl.
In this patch of whimsy, sing,
With magic found in every spring.

Tangles of Hope and Heritage

Amidst the vines of stories old,
Woven threads where dreams unfold.
Sneaky squirrels trade ancient tales,
While laughter rides the gentle gales.

Roots that tangle, giggles spark,
Whispers hidden in the dark.
Grannies nod, with knowing grins,
As mischief brews where fun begins.

Mossy pillows, perfect for naps,
Silly gnomes with fuzzy caps.
Share a chuckle, hear the cheer,
Every joke, a hidden leer.

So gather 'round, both young and old,
In tangled stories, be so bold.
Laughter bonds, like roots of trees,
Inherit joy, share your tease.

The Forest of Daydreams

In a realm where giggles grow,
A canopy of dreams bestow.
Silly shadows, a twisty race,
Chasing laughter, find your place.

Mirthful echoes through the trees,
Whirling with the buzzing bees.
Swinging high on branches bright,
Giggles bounce in pure delight.

Puppies prance on puffs of cloud,
Whispering secrets, cheerful, loud.
Chasing whispers, surprises pop,
Every stumble, a giggly flop.

Close your eyes, and watch it soar,
Imagined worlds forevermore.
Let the whimsy take a leap,
In daydreams' arms, find joy to keep.

Secrets Under the Leafy Arch

Beneath leaves that sway and sway,
Hide the mischief of the day.
Giggling crickets, full of schemes,
Plotting dances, living dreams.

Breezes blow through giggling trees,
Whispering jokes with playful ease.
Silly shadows, a hide and seek,
Mischief blossoms, laughter peaks.

Dancing roots and tickled toes,
Under arches, fun just flows.
Squeaky frogs make raucous cheer,
Join the fun, don't disappear!

Secrets shared in quiet glades,
With every chuckle, joy cascades.
A leafy arch of joy so grand,
Brings the playful dreamers hand in hand.

Clusters of Green Reverie

In a garden where giggles bloom,
Plants wear hats, free from gloom.
Lizards dance, quite out of line,
Mischief sprouts with each vine.

Pillows of moss, a soft delight,
They jump and bounce with sheer might.
Snails have races, slow and grand,
In this whimsical, greenish land.

Bumblebees hum a cheerful tune,
While butterflies juggle with the moon.
Chasing shadows, they spin and twirl,
As laughter lifts around the whirl.

So join this crazy leafy spree,
When the flowers nod in glee.
With every twist and joyful cheer,
Nature's laughter fills the sphere.

The Garden of Forgotten Dreams

In a plot where lost thoughts lay,
Dirt is sprinkled with ballet.
Wind whispers secrets, oh so loud,
As sleepy heads uncurl from cloud.

A scarecrow dons a silly hat,
While weeds gossip, 'Who's that brat?'
Garden gnomes have tea at four,
Clattering cups, such a chore!

Sunflowers boast of heights so tall,
While tiny ants prepare their ball.
Petunias giggle, sway, and spin,
In this bright realm where dreams begin.

Stars above wink with delight,
As nighttime sprinkles soft, gentle light.
And here in this whimsical theme,
Lies a garden of a grander dream.

The Sylvan Serenade

Trees play music with their leaves,
As playful critters dance in eaves.
A squirrel's joke, a chipmunk's trick,
In the woods, time travels thick.

Caterpillars pen a play,
With ladybugs as cast all day.
Fun in shade, they plot and scheme,
In this magical woodland dream.

Foxes leap with graceful flair,
While raccoons strut without a care.
Whispers of laughter fill the night,
As moonbeams catch the frolic light.

So join this merry woodland tune,
Where every creature's in a swoon.
In the groves, where laughter's spun,
Nature's marvels weigh a ton.

Fronds in the Moonlight

Amid the night, shadows unfold,
Whispers of tales in green, retold.
Fronds sway like dancers, limbs all carefree,
Mischief is brewing under the tree.

With giggles echoing through the dark,
A raccoon picks up its trademark.
Napping owls squawk a funny tune,
As the breeze croons to the moon.

Fireflies twinkle in a light parade,
While frogs croak jokes unafraid.
In the hush, the woodland plays,
Where laughter lingers for days.

So come and dance with nature's crew,
In this surreal rendezvous.
Where every leaf might speak a jest,
And nighttime revelry is the best.

Secrets of the Woodland Realm

In the woods where whispers dwell,
A squirrel's dance just fits the spell.
With acorns tossed in playful glee,
Nature's jesters weave their spree.

A mushroom wears a tiny hat,
A rabbit thinks he's very fat.
With giggles hid in leafy seams,
The forest plays in silly dreams.

A badger skids on mossy ground,
While hedgehogs cheer with laughter sound.
The twilight shimmers with delight,
As shadows giggle, hide from sight.

With twinkling eyes and cheeky grins,
The woodland knows where fun begins.
Amidst the trees, no need to hide,
In every nook, pure joy resides.

Moss and Mirth

Upon the stones, a jolly crew,
The mossy carpet, vibrant hue.
A snail slides by with style so grand,
While beetles boast of grand, cool plans.

The chipmunk sings a silly tune,
Beneath the light of a chubby moon.
While fireflies dance in twinkling show,
The night reveals a lighthearted glow.

A frog holds court on a lily pad,
Spinning tales that make all glad.
The croaks and chirps in harmony,
In this green tale, joy is key.

With laughter echoing through the glade,
The woodland dreams are brightly made.
And gatherings of critters unite,
In mirthful games until the night.

Enigma of the Green Veil

Behind the leaves, a riddle plays,
As dandelions sway and sway.
A hedgehog pranks the passing breeze,
With funny faces that aim to please.

A whisper stirs the dewy ferns,
Where giggles rise with sly concerns.
The shadows chuckle in a chase,
As laughter twirls with lively grace.

The owls pretend to be quite wise,
Yet wink at clouds and playful flies.
The mysteries of green unfold,
With joyous tales just waiting to be told.

So stroll along where secrets hide,
With every twist, let joy collide.
For nature's jest is all around,
In every turn, pure fun is found.

The Enchanted Thicket's Lullaby

In a thicket where giggles sleep,
The foliage leans in, secrets to keep.
A fox in pajamas, what a sight,
Dreaming of cheese in the soft moonlight.

Beneath the boughs of ancient trees,
Squirrels debate the best of cheese.
While ladybugs share tales of flight,
The stars above give wink just right.

A rabbit jumps up, takes a bow,
Declaring he's the funniest of all now.
With every hop, a laugh takes wing,
In woodland courts, they dance and sing.

The leaves chuckle, the branches sway,
In this enchanted, whimsical array.
As twilight falls, the dreams take flight,
Bringing joy to this starry night.

Celestial Blooms Amongst Shadows

In the twilight where mischief grows,
Petals giggle, and the moonlight glows.
Caterpillars dance in a wobbly line,
Whispering secrets, oh, isn't it fine?

The stars above with a twinkle so bright,
Watch the toadstools host a grand night flight.
Frogs wear top hats, and fireflies cheer,
While shadows play tag with a hint of a sneer.

Joking plants recite their leafy jest,
As bumbling bees put their skills to the test.
"Oh dear!" they buzz, "we forgot the way,
To the royal nectar buffet we must sway."

Beneath the echo of laughter clear,
Amidst tangled whispers, there's no room for fear.
Come join the fun in this leafy domain,
Where each step is wacky and joy will remain.

Reveries of the Shaded Path

Along the path where shadows prance,
Dancing mushrooms invite a chance.
A squirrel in shades holds a tiny drink,
Sipping on acorns, what do you think?

A bashful raccoon wearing a grin,
Laughs at the way the hedgehogs spin.
"The world is round, but we're rather flat,
Who knew living life could be such a chat?"

Giggling grasses tickle toes,
As wanderers trip on the path's highs and lows.
But laughter echoes when they fall,
"Get up! Quick! Don't miss the ball!"

With each twist and turn of the winding trail,
Unexpected antics begin to prevail.
Come join the reveries under the leaves,
Where humor flourishes and joy never cleaves.

The Hidden Melody of the Forest

In the deep woods where the giggles hum,
A chorus of critters makes quite the sum.
Owls wearing glasses compose silly songs,
As the wind chimes in with delightful prongs.

Fungi convene for their weekly show,
Casting shadows where the kind breezes blow.
"I'm a ballet star," quips a stout toad,
As he leaps high, landing near the road.

Crickets play tunes from dusk until dawn,
While hedgehogs roll over, quite far from their lawn.
"Do a cartwheel! Show us your flair!"
They cheer and they chortle, devoid of a care.

Every rustle and shuffle in this melodic hub,
Creates an orchestra of giggles and rub.
So join the delight where nature's expressed,
And bring a joke, we're all humor-obsessed!

Enigmas in the Underwood

Beneath the canopy of green delight,
Curious tales develop in the night.
Mice in capes spin capricious schemes,
While the moon winks and conjures dreams.

"Why did the squirrel bring a suitcase?"
It chuckled and twirled in a nutcase race.
With every misstep, laughter erupts,
Even the best laid plans get corrupted.

A fox wearing socks pulls a funny face,
"How does it feel to be out of place?"
Tumbling thickets of humor and woe,
In this underwood, the fun will grow.

Puns quicken the heart in this secret nook,
Where each squirrel's tale is a comic book.
So wander beneath this playful guise,
Where the enigmas arise with bright, twinkling eyes.

Lush Reveries in Greener Realms

In a glade where giggles grow,
The leaves weave tales of absurdity,
A frog dons a crown of leafy glow,
Claiming he's king of all things silly.

A squirrel in shades, quite the sight,
Dances with the shadows of trees,
He twirls and spins, much to delight,
Drawing laughter on the summer breeze.

The mushrooms hold a grand soirée,
Where ants perform a tap dance spree,
Each sprout sings in its quirky way,
As magic whispers in jubilee.

Beneath the boughs where humor thrives,
Lies a tapestry of jovial cheer,
Where giggling critters lead their lives,
In green realms of whimsy, far and near.

Celestial Growth in Twilight Groves

As twilight paints the world in gold,
The shadows deepen, mischief starts,
A rabbit's tale, playfully bold,
Of stolen carrots and fledgling smarts.

The moon winks down with silver glee,
A dandelion dons a starry hat,
It whispers secrets to a bumblebee,
While crickets chirp a funny chat.

A hedgehog seeks a starlit dream,
That twinkles with a giggling sprite,
Who dances in the night's soft gleam,
On wings of laughter, pure delight.

At twilight's end, giggles abide,
In growths enchanted, ever spry,
Where whimsy reigns and joys collide,
In moonlit pastures, none ask why.

Echoes of Nature's Illusions

The breeze carries whispers of cheer,
As mushrooms wear hats like top-liners,
With each rustle, laughter draws near,
When butterflies play as tiny miners.

A snail disputes with a firefly,
Claiming the best glow in the park,
They battle it out with a wink of an eye,
While frogs croon their tunes after dark.

In the underbrush, a riddle brews,
As crickets hold court in moonlit mirth,
Each creature boasts of what it can do,
In a riotous show of earthy worth.

Echoes dance where humor prevails,
In every nook, a chuckle you'll find,
Where nature spins her whimsical tales,
And imagination runs unconfined.

Fernwood Fables

In a thicket where stories sprout,
Entwined with laughter, wild and bright,
A rabbit hops with a playful shout,
Avoiding traps of leaves just right.

A caterpillar shares a dream,
Of flying high with wings so grand,
But falls asleep by a bubbling stream,
Snoring tales of a wandering band.

The blossoms giggle in the sun,
As shadows play a lively game,
In every bloom, a joke is spun,
Humor woven like a gentle flame.

In ferny woods, where giggles thrive,
Fables emerge from every glade,
In this realm, all creatures come alive,
With chuckles sweet and mischief made.

The Veil of Ancient Greens

In the forest's secret nook,
Where leaves play hide and seek,
The fancies of the sprouting life,
Are giggling in their peek.

With critters dressed in leafy shrouds,
They host a grand charade,
A revelry of whispers soft,
Beneath the amber shade.

Laughter tickles every stem,
As creatures twirl and leap,
They plot to steal the sunlight,
And cozy-up to sleep.

Why not join their merry spree?
A crown of vines to wear,
With a hat made of mushrooms,
You'll be the star, I swear!

A Realm of Perpetual Sprout

In a kingdom of the green so bright,
The sprouts are full of glee,
They joke about the snoozing buds,
And giggle 'til the tea.

They hold a court of tiny bugs,
With crowns of dew and lace,
Debating who has the finest fronds,
While planning a sprinting race.

A snail slips on the damp, thick slime,
And earns a round of cheer,
For every slip and spin they take,
Adds more to the grand veneer.

So grab your shoes of muddy soil,
And join this leafy crew,
For who would miss such silly fun,
In this emerald avenue?

Hidden Worlds in the Wilderness

In a wild and leafy realm,
Where shadows chase the light,
Tiny creatures make their homes,
In havens out of sight.

A pixie fluffs her mossy bed,
With giggles that resound,
While dancing to the wobbly tunes,
Of the mushrooms all around.

They build a castle out of twigs,
And hold a feast for sprites,
With fruit from clouds, and nectar drops,
They toast to silly rites.

Come peek beneath the emerald canopies,
Where laughter grows like weeds,
In this hidden, funny land,
Where absurdity succeeds!

The Dance of the Mossy Spirits

When twilight drapes the forest floor,
And all seems calm and still,
The spirits of the moss arise,
With mischief in their thrill.

They swirl and twirl with every breeze,
While humming tunes of cheer,
A parade of shades and giggles,
That only we can hear.

Now keep your eyes on starlit paths,
As they bounce from fern to fern,
For if you catch them in the act,
You'll learn what they discern.

So join the waltz of vibrant green,
With laughter as your guide,
For in this merry woodland dance,
Your heart will swell with pride!

Ethereal Paths of Green

In a world where plants wear hats,
And mushrooms dance like acrobats.
Grass tickles toes in playful glee,
As critters laugh, oh can't you see?

A squirrel spins tales of grand delight,
With acorns clinking, what a sight!
The leaves whisper jokes, oh so sly,
While butterflies twirl and float on by.

The shadows stretch, the sunlight beams,
Causing trees to giggle in dreams.
Every step brings a chuckle near,
As nature's jesters fill our ear.

So take a stroll on this green spree,
Join the dance of the leafy spree.
The paths of whimsy lead the way,
In this realm where laughter plays.

The Lure of Shaded Glades

In hidden nooks where laughter grows,
The sunlight tickles the leaves like prose.
Mice in tuxedos sneak up for tea,
While wise old owls hoot, 'Come join me!'

Beneath the ferns, a party brews,
With grasshoppers jamming to old-time blues.
Crickets play cards, you can join the game,
The stakes are high – your first name's the fame!

A raccoon juggles some acorn snacks,
While rabbits plot their next funny act.
The trees sway gently, as if they grin,
In this shady glade where joy can't thin.

So come and linger, leave worries behind,
In this realm where humor's never confined.
The shadows invite you to laugh and prance,
In the glades where whimsy leads the dance.

Secrets of the Forest Floor

Down below where the soft moss lies,
The tiny critters share their wise ties.
Ants in a line form a conga line,
While snails make slime, oh how divine!

A fox tells tales of grand escapades,
While beetles boast of their shiny parades.
A worm recites poems without any fuss,
Yet all sit quiet when the owl makes a fuss.

Beneath thick roots where whispers creep,
The secrets bloom while frogs prattle deep.
They chuckle softly at clumsy falls,
As nature giggles and endlessly calls.

So venture down to this joyful lore,
Where laughter's hidden on the forest floor.
With every step, the silliness grows,
In the heart of the woods where the humor flows.

Fantasies in the Fernshade

In the cool hush of leafy embrace,
A gnome sits grinning; just watch his face.
With pixies twirling in glittery shoes,
They play hide and seek with the warm morning dew.

A hedgehog dons a shiny pink hat,
While beetles compete in a dance-off spat.
The flowers giggle at the funny show,
As daisies wink, in their pretty row.

Giggling squirrels race up the trees,
Aloud with chirps of humorous tease.
The sunlight filters, a golden stream,
Bathing all in a whimsical dream.

So join the fun in this ferny glen,
Where laughter's a chorus, and joy's a pen.
Let your heart wander and find your place,
In the shade of fancies, where smiles embrace.

Echoes Among Twisting Vines

In conga lines the leaves do sway,
With critters dancing, come what may.
A frog with socks, a sly raccoon,
They groove beneath the silver moon.

Bouncing beetles join the spree,
While butterflies sip herbal tea.
A squirrel in shades, he takes the stage,
Reciting jokes from a tiny page.

Laughter ripples through the air,
As wildflowers spin without a care.
A chorus of giggles, sweet and bright,
As shadows twinkle in the night.

In this realm where whimsy thrives,
The vines echo with joyful lives.
Adventure waits in every twist,
In leafy realms, you can't resist.

The Wandering Spirit of the Grove.

There's a sprite with sparkling shoes,
Swapping tales of morning blues.
He nibbles on a wiggly root,
Then challenges a crow to a hoot-to-hoo.

Behind the trees, they play charades,
Where shadows hide in leaf-made glades.
A mushroom cap, a funny hat,
As squirrels giggle, 'What's up with that?'

The wandering spirit jigs with glee,
Inviting all to come and see.
A parade of paws, a flurry of tails,
In this forest of absurd details.

With each rustling breeze, a wink, a grin,
Magic flourishes like the sun's warm spin.
In the grove where laughter flows,
Joyful souls come and dance in rows.

Whispers of the Woodland

Beneath the ferns where shadows tease,
A pickle jar lost among the trees.
Insects rave and throw a ball,
The tiniest critters, having a brawl.

Mice in tutus, foxes in ties,
A party where no one complies.
With acorns raising their tiny fists,
In the woodlands where oddity persists.

A snail with dreams of grandeur sways,
While the thunderous stomp of a deer delays.
'Don't step here!' the tiny creatures shout,
As he struggles to dance, but wiggles about.

The whispers call for silliness near,
In this land where laughter's the highest cheer.
With every giggle, the woodland glows,
And what's beyond is anyone's guess.

Elves Beneath the Canopy

Under the boughs, in outfits bright,
Elves play pranks from day to night.
With mischief tucked in every pocket,
They twist and whirl like a wild rocket.

A caper here, a trip down there,
Turning stones into chairs for air.
A dragonfly steals a glittery shoe,
While they giggle and shout, 'Is that really you?'

With laughter echoing like tiny bells,
Their stories told in laughter spells.
Sprinkling giggles in dew-soaked air,
Beneath the leaves, there's joy to share.

The antics grow into the night,
With moonlit dances, oh what a sight!
Where elves with whims and dreams galore,
Create a magic night forevermore.

Fern-laden Echoes

In a jungle of green, they weave and they sway,
Gossiping tales in a peculiar way.
They tickle the toes of the wandering shoe,
"Come dance with us, won't you? We're quite the crew!"

A rabbit hopped by, with a top hat on straight,
"Do join our party, we'll celebrate fate!"
A squirrel stood by, with acorns to spend,
"The punchline is nuts, you'll laugh 'til the end!"

The breeze in the leaves sang a whimsical tune,
The shadows all chuckled, by light of the moon.
With twirls and with flips, they all joined the spree,
"Who knew that a brush would feel so carefree!"

So if you should wander where the oddities roam,
Beware of the laughter; you'll want to come home.
They'll coax out your giggles with every soft rustle,
In the land of the joyful, where whimsy's a hustle.

Emerald Myths of the Silent Wood

In the heart of the grove where secrets reside,
Stood a gnome named Gary with each lie amplified.
"I once rode a dragon!" he'd boast with a grin,
While the squirrels rolled their eyes, absorbed in their kin.

The trees held their laughter, their trunks trembling tight,
As Gary spun stories from morning till night.
"I wooed a green fairy with charm and with cheer,
But she fled with a leaf, just to keep it unclear!"

A raccoon chimed in, with a smirk on his face,
"Oh Gary, you dreamer, in your trippy place!"
With a flick of his tail, he joined in the jest,
"Your tales are so tall, they could almost be blessed!"

So remember dear wanderers, in woodlands so deep,
Where green comes alive and the legends just leap.
The laughter that lingers, the myths made of light,
Will have you believing by the end of the night.

Tales from the Whispering Path

On the whispering path, with secrets to share,
A hedgehog named Henry wore a bright pink flair.
He chuckled and snickered with each little stride,
"I bet I can race you, the shrubs are my guide!"

A rabbit with style, in high-top white shoes,
Joined the silly footrace, declaring, "No blues!"
With sprigs of fresh thyme, they zipped and they zoomed,

As the flowers all giggled, the garden consumed.

Then came a wise owl with spectacles round,
"What chaos is this? Is there trouble around?"
With a wink and a hoot, the grand dame took flight,
"Let's hold a soirée, it'll surely ignite!"

So gather your friends, in this leafy retreat,
Where laughter's the music, and fun's quite a feat.
As shadows grow long, and the stars start to peek,
The whispers of joy are the sounds that you seek.

Shadows and Secrets of the Thicket

In shadows so thick, where the odd creatures lurk,
A dapper old fox played a sly little perk.
With his tales of the night, he'd gather them round,
"I transformed into mist, does that seem so profound?"

A badger would snort and roll over with glee,
"Oh Fox, with your tricks, you could set my mind free!"
The night critters giggled, their secrets unspooled,
With a pinch of delight, their imaginations fueled.

Tiny bats hanging upside-down like a dream,
Whispered sweet stories, like a whimsical scheme.
"We saw dancing flowers that could sing a real tune,
They'd waltz in the night 'neath the light of the moon!"

So if you should wander through thickets of chatter,
Take pause by the shadows; listen to their clatter.
For each leaf has a tale, a chuckle divine,
In the thicket of laughter, everything's fine!

Sylvan Serenades and Dappled Light

In the woods, where critters prance,
A squirrel in tu-tus starts to dance,
The rabbits giggle, sharing snacks,
While hedgehogs don their festive hats.

Butterflies wearing bowties fly,
Telling jokes as they flutter by,
"You think you're slow? Just take a seat,
We're all just here for something sweet!"

The trees hum tunes with leafy glee,
While ants form lines for a jamboree,
With acorns rolling to the beat,
Join in the fun, won't miss a treat!

So if you wander through this place,
Prepare to join the merry race,
With nature's whimsy all around,
You'll find that laughter's always found!

The Otherworldly Grove

In a grove where shadows play,
The gnomes throw parties every day,
They dance with mushrooms, spin with glee,
And serve confetti made of leaves.

A pixie flies with mismatched socks,
Juggling acorns, tickling rocks,
"Who's got the sprout?" she loudly cries,
"Just don't forget the lemon pies!"

A troll in pajamas takes a nap,
While fairies weave a magic map,
It leads to places that are fun,
A silly realm where jokes are spun!

So venture forth and join the cheer,
In this realm, there's nothing to fear,
With whimsy wrapped in leafy folds,
You'll uncover stories yet untold!

Verdant Whispers in the Mist

In the mist, the whispers flow,
Of dandelions putting on a show,
Little bugs with tiny hats,
Tell tall tales of acrobats.

A talking fern plays hide and seek,
With beetles rolling on their cheeks,
"Come join our game!" they giggle loud,
As shadows dance beneath the cloud.

The toads recite their rhyming prayers,
While foxes tease without a care,
In this slick, enchanted plot,
Where silly tales are all they've got!

So leap and twirl, and don't be shy,
Join the laughter 'neath the sky,
In the mist where dreams collide,
With fables sprouting side by side!

Chasing Shadows Through the Thicket

Through the thicket, shadows chase,
With wiggly lines in a silly race,
A rabbit trips on thistle stems,
Whilst owls cheer with bright "Whoo" gems!

A mouse employs a funky tune,
As he jives beneath the moon,
"Why are you running?" asks a lark,
"Just after shadows—remember the spark!"

The bushes giggle, swaying round,
As critters join the jumbled sound,
Pinecones roll like bowling balls,
While laughter echoes through the halls.

So grab a friend, and run about,
In the thicket, we'll laugh and shout,
For every turn, there's joy to find,
In this silly, playful kind!

The Luminous Glade

In the glade where shadows play,
Frogs declare it's opera day.
With silly hats and leaps so grand,
They croak their notes, a quirky band.

Fireflies dance with twinkling lights,
Mounting on mushrooms, a carnival of sights.
A rabbit slips in a dance-off spree,
Who knew hops could bring such glee?

Squirrels slide on leafy slides,
Competing who can take the widest strides.
Their acorn helmets bounce with style,
Oh, to join them for a while!

As twilight paints the sky with hues,
The critters gather, spread the news.
In this gleeful, glowing scene,
Laughter reigns, it's quite the dream.

Aspirations of the Wild

In a forest brimming with delight,
A snail dreams of speed, a comical sight.
"I'll race the hare," he shouts with glee,
But the hare just chuckles, "Oh, let it be!"

A rascally raccoon dons a mask,
In nighttime heists, he takes to the task.
Stealing snacks from folks nearby,
But trips on branches and flops with a sigh.

The wise old owl with a book in tow,
Claims to know all, but just puts on a show.
Trying to teach squirrel the art of math,
But ends up in a baffling path!

Though they fumble and often jest,
The joy in wild antics is always the best.
They dance under stars, all full of cheer,
Laughter alive in the atmosphere.

Veils of the Verdant Realm

Amidst the leaves, a dance begins,
With grins so wide, the mischief spins.
A hedgehog twirls in a grass-made dress,
While bumblebees buzz, I must confess.

Worms in top hats, wiggling with flair,
Fancy moves earned with much care.
The groundhogs cheer, making a scene,
While a caterpillar practices to be lean.

A party of frogs, in tuxedos neat,
Croaking serenades, a dapper treat.
In this theater amongst glades and blooms,
Even the sun chuckles, brightening rooms.

Laughter echoes, whispers take flight,
In this vibrant world, such a silly sight.
As songbirds sing their raucous rhymes,
Frolics abound, in joyous chimes.

Echoes of the Sylphs

Beneath the boughs, where fairies roam,
Their giggles echo, calling it home.
A gnome attempts a grand charade,
But trips on roots, in a flailing parade.

The sylphs painted with glimmering dust,
Create mischief, because they must.
They swap the hats of unsuspecting friends,
Embracing the laughs, where silliness blends.

A porcupine in a tutu spins,
While a bunny plays fiddle, oh how it grins!
With every note, the wild things sway,
Creating joy in a whimsical way.

As twilight blankets the merry scene,
They join in a jig, proud and serene.
Chasing dreams within the night,
With laughter that echoes until the light.

www.ingramcontent.com/pod-product-compliance
Lightning Source LLC
Chambersburg PA
CBHW070309120526
44590CB00017B/2596